Simply stated, Dr John South is the best Chaplain, I have ever served with in 28 total years of combined active and reserve service in the United States Army. As a Chaplain in the USAR, he was highly respected and sought after for his caring counsel and his pristine reputation. He was known for his ability to relate to soldiers and provide invaluable counseling based in spiritual principles. Again, simply the best!"

Randie O'Neal

Chaplain South's book comes along at the precise time it is needed. With so many military members retuning from combat facing PTSD, severe physical and emotional wounds and a high rate of suicide, this book brings answers. Chaplain South has lived with all of these situations personally. He uses his faith in his own crisis survival and has helped many others as they have faced crisis and devastation. He has been called in many times by the FBI, ATF and the U.S. Army to help in tragic situations such as Columbine High School shootings and the attack on the World Trade Center on 9/11. During all of these events, Chaplain South offers hope, love and compassion to survivors.

Stephen Fry

I first met John South during a very horrifying time in my life. On September 11, 2001, my brother, New York City Police Officer Walter Weaver, was killed in the World Trade Center attack. Crisis counselors were called in from all over the country to assist family members during such a grievous time. Into my life walked John South, not your typical-looking Chaplin. While I do not recall if he had a white collar on, I could sense immediately he was a messenger of God and there to help. Over the next few weeks we met daily, went to lunch and dinner, and talked about a wide variety of topics. I quickly saw that John was a good man with plenty of substance and someone who truly cared about easing pain and caring for hurt individuals. As time passed, my wounds scabbed over and John went back to Arizona. We kept in touch via text and email. I know he was instrumental in my healing, with his devotion to seeing me through such a horrific event. I now am proud to say John is a dear friend and I can't wait to read this book. The world needs more people like John South.

Brian J Weaver

As a nine-year volunteer chaplain for the Bureau of Alcohol, Tobacco, Firearms and Explosives, Chaplain South has consistently exhibited concern, compassion, and a true willingness to go the extra mile. He assisted our peer support teams in Colorado in 1999 after the Columbine shootings, worked with the many ATF employees and their families affected by the 9/11 tragedy in NYC, and participated in briefings for ATF Special Agents and Explosives Specialists deployed to Iraq to assist the Iraqi military, police force and government. Chaplain South is a person dedicated to all that is honorable and good.

Marianne Ketels, Ombudsman,
Bureau of Alcohol, Tobacco, Firearms and Explosives

Had it not been for the dedication and devotion of Chaplain John South, the Weaver family would not have emotionally survived the catastrophe of 9/11. His faith and understanding has given our family the ability to remain strong in spite of losing Walter. It was Chaplain South who always reminded us that Walter was doing what he loved.
John DiStephano

I really enjoyed your story. It will help many on many levels and for many different reasons.
"Harv"

I wanted to let you know that I experienced such a feeling of hope and peace after reading his book. I'm sure that many people will be helped by it.
"Martie Lou"

I've read nearly all of your book. Amazing stuff. It's a book I need to read again. Thanks for writing it.
Fred Stone

Your book is a blessing ... a treasure! The ability to articulate with clarity the Hope you have in your heart is the most touching! It is throughout the book — the bottom line of the message. I felt it pour forth so that it can touch the hearts of those who need it so much. Thank you for sharing with such honest and openness.
Sister Georjean - Canaan in the Desert

A Journey Through

PTSD

by

Dr. (Chaplain) John J. South

A Journey through PTSD
© 2015 John South
All rights reserved

ISBN: 978-0-9965066-0-1

Book & cover design by Dee Dees

Published by
LifeGuides Press
Mesa, AZ 85209
480 703-1244

Printed in the United States of America

DEDICATION

This book is dedicated first to my mother, Louise E. South, who was my protector—often at her own peril. She was my physical savior, and the one who first instilled in me a love of God. She was the epitome of perseverance, steadfastness, courage and faith, even through our darkest times.

AND IN MEMORY OF ...

NYPD Officer Walter Weaver and all the other law enforcement officers and firefighters who lost their lives while helping victims of the tragedy on 9/11.

ACKNOWLEDGEMENTS

I first must thank my wife, Nita, for standing by me, understanding, and helping me through the dark times of my life. Without her, I don't know where I would be today.

I'm so thankful for all my children and grandchildren, and grateful for their ongoing, loving support and prayers. They, too, have made life worth living.

So many people have given me support and encouragement in all areas of my life, and I can never name them all. But I do want to acknowledge a few here who particularly encouraged me to write this book, and supported me during the process.

The first was Dr. Earl Radmacher, who was President of Western Seminary when I attended in 1982. In one of his classes, I was required to write a 25 page thesis of my life. When it was finished, he encouraged me to someday write a book about my life and God's part in it.

Dr. Luis Palau also read the thesis and encouraged me to write the full story. He is a great man of God.

Since moving to Phoenix and becoming involved in the Army Chaplaincy, two of my bosses, MG John L. Scott and MG Paul Mock suggested I write my story, and include information about PTSD and Crisis/Suicide Intervention.

The need for a book like this has also been brought home to me by all the soldiers I've talked to over the years, who have told me there is nothing available that delves into the real needs of soldiers (dealing with crisis, family, marriage, suicide, PTSD, who to call, how to call, and basic information.) Many said they were tired of the "head-strong psychologist" talk, and wanted some real-life applications. Their needs and honest, straight-talk, encouraged me to get this book done for them, and others like them.

Marcel Lanter (called "Mom" by all at the Phoenix Army Reserve unit,) not only brought coffee, fruit and goodies to every drill for over 20 years, but she was a strong soldier of Christ, and prayed about the idea of this book long before it was begun.

Marcel's son, Robert Rehm, was in Vietnam, remained in the reserve all his life, and retired as an Arizona Highway Patrol Officer. He too, has always been a good prayer buddy for me.

Thanks to my friends, Dee and Fred Dees, who supported and encouraged me during the 18 months of writing this, and for Dee's editing and guidance to make the book a reality.

Thanks so much to my life-long—and best—friends, Bob and Sheila Blecksmith, who have been my biggest cheerleaders since my early days in law enforcement.

Finally, and most importantly, all the direction for this book came from my real Commander-in-Chief, Jesus Christ.

TABLE OF CONTENTS

INTRODUCTION

Through nearly 50 years of serving in the military, law enforcement, and as a chaplain, I have seen more than my share of death and devastation, and I've dealt with the aftermath of both. I'm convinced that the real victims are often not those who died, but those who survived.

Whether it be soldiers who have returned from the battlefields, police officers who have witnessed the brutality of murder and the horror of tragic auto accidents, or surviving victims of violent crime, all can suffer the often debilitating effects of depression and PTSD.

These two conditions are insidious because they are often misunderstood by the victims themselves and are sometimes hidden or kept under wraps. Even after they've been diagnosed, the disorders are not understood—and sometimes not accepted— by those around them. Family members insist the sufferer "snap out of it," and when that doesn't happen, they often desert; physically or emotionally.

In Part I of this book, I hope to demonstrate how these symptoms often come to be, by sharing my own experiences; abuse as a child, a traumatic war injury, the devastating loss of a career I loved, and the horror I saw at Columbine and during the 9/11 recovery efforts.

Part II deals with how depression and PTSD manifest themselves, and what help is needed to treat victims.

I hope my experiences and what I've learned both as a sufferer of PTSD and depression, as well as one who strives to help others who also live with either or both of these conditions, can provide some understanding and guidance for those who either suffer themselves, live with or know someone who does, or are in a position to help those individuals.

Dr. (Chaplain) John South

FOREWORD

Chaplain John South is uniquely qualified to provide assistance for those who suffer from Post Traumatic Stress Disorder. With a troubled childhood and the severe physical and mental wounds from serving in Vietnam, his more than 35 years of service as a chaplain in various military and police environments have allowed him to write this compelling and relevant book. Dr. South provides unique insights into PTSD, and I can attest that during his 20+ years serving the men and women of the Phoenix Police Department, many of whom have suffered trauma and its after-effects, hundreds have been the beneficiaries of his knowledge and skills.

This book creates a legacy for Dr. South while providing support to those on the journey through PTSD. In the two decades I have known John, I never cease to be amazed by his dedication to soldiers and police officers. His desire to assist in any way he can to prevent harmful behavior and suicides of those who have given so much to our communities, locally, nationally and internationally, comes from his faith and passion to help.

Chaplain John South has personally suffered not only the effects of combat wounds and PTSD, but the lingering and devastating after-effects of "agent orange." His unfailing faith in God, his deep educational preparation, and his belief in others has allowed him the strength to carry on for a higher purpose. His courage and journey are inspirational for all.

Chief (Retired) Jack Harris
Phoenix Police Department

PART

I

Prologue

August 25, 1966
Vietnam

My buddy Eddy and I were walking away from the APC when small-arms fire suddenly erupted around us. I spun around and looked behind Eddy. My mind barely registered a bright flash and a puff of smoke beforeI was knocked into the air and landed on my back. I had been shot.

A dust-off helicopter landed and I was loaded into the left side of the Huey. Eddy was being lifted into the other side. My left shoulder was a bloody stump. I kept telling Eddy to hang on—we were going to make it.

When the Huey landed at the aid station north of Lai Khe, I looked over at Eddy to reassure him we'd be okay now. But when they lifted him off the gurney, daylight shone through a huge gap where his heart should have been. I knew he was dead. I would later learn that we had both been hit by the same machine-gun round.

A doctor started an IV and stopped my bleeding, while telling me that I had a severe wound and could consider myself fortunate to be alive. I was flown to Ben Hoa 7th Field Hospital, near Saigon, where I was rushed into surgery and doctors repaired the muscle and tissue damage to my shoulder.

After a month in Saigon I was transferred to the 249th General Hospital in Osaka, Japan for skin grafts. I'd spend the next three-and-a-half months recovering there.

I had arrived in Vietnam not caring whether I lived or died. Now I desperately wanted to survive. And I knew God was working in my life. The months I spent in Osaka gave me the time I needed to reflect on my life so far ... and what my future might hold.

Dust-off helicopter

1

A Rough Beginning

Louise South - My Mom

My childhood could only be described as filled with strife and anger. I always thought it might have turned out differently if my biological father had not walked out on us right after my birth. But he did, and everything changed.

My mother's life had not been an easy one. Her father too, had left the family and taken everything when Mom was a young girl. Her mother—left with nothing, and trying to survive the Great Depression—struggled to take care of her daughter. When Mom was twelve, her older brother took her in until their mother could get on her feet and get settled again. He raised his little sister for the next five years, but he had an overprotective and fearful nature, so it was not always a happy place to live. What few happy times she had during those years occurred when Mom had the opportunity to be a back-up singer with the gospel group, The Stamps Quartet, in Arkansas. She sang with them until she was seventeen.

When Mom was in twelfth grade, her mother was able to bring her back home. Grandma was an industrious and determined woman, and had managed to start a department store in Arkansas, which prospered and eventually provided a good life for her family.

During WWII, Mom enlisted in the Army Air Corp. She became an assistant to one of the unit flight commanders, and for a while she worked for Gene Autry, the cowboy movie star and singer. She admired him because he was a solid Christian, and he was respectful of women in the Air Force. Mom was thrilled when she once had the opportunity to fly with him in his well-known B-24 Liberator.

Early in 1944, Mom met my biological father, John Miller. They married later that year, and I came along in October, 1945. Before I was two years old, my father had divorced Mom and walked out of our lives. A couple of factors probably contributed his decision.

Mom and Me, 1946

From what I've been told, his family were wealthy Catholics who threatened to disown him if he didn't leave my mother. They refused to accept their union, since my parents were not married in the Catholic Church. However, I don't think it was the church that was against the marriage, as much as it was him hiding behind the church. In addition to his family's

6

disapproval was John Miller's desire to go to flight school. When he and Mom were married, Miller was a Master Sergeant, but had a strong desire to fly. In those days, only single men were accepted as candidates for flight school.

Between his quest to become a pilot and the pressure and influence from his family, John Miller took the easy way out. He divorced my mother, leaving me behind in his wake. My mom really loved him and his desertion broke her heart.

I learned all of this as a teenager, and it disturbed me that he could walk away from his young wife and child with no apparent remorse. It hurt that he never made any effort to contact me in my formative years. By then I was looking for someone to rescue me, and I always hoped it might be him. My grandmother knew of his whereabouts, but she was very secretive about him. She told me that he was wealthy, a test pilot for Lockheed, and had remarried and had three children.

After he left, Mom and I moved back in with Grandma, and Mom got a job in a shoe store. It was there she met Earnest Milton South, who had grown up on a farm in Arkansas. His father, Joe, was a mean drunk who would often beat his son with a switch and razor strap, and made him quit school after the third grade to work on the farm. In later years, when Joe came to visit us, he seemed meek and friendly, but when he was drunk, it was a different story.

Earnest South also appeared to be kind and gentle in the beginning, and Mom soon married him to make a home for me. She felt she needed to get away from living with her mother, as Grandma was very opinionated and controlling. Our new little family moved to the Flint/Detroit area of Michigan, and both my parents went to work for Chevrolet. Earnest was soon made a foreman and was making good money, though Mom and I saw very little of it. When I was five, Earnest legally adopted me, though I've often wondered why.

My stepfather was a cruel, uneducated, alcoholic factory worker who was verbally and physically abusive to my mother and me while I was growing up. We lived in fear, never knowing what his mood would be from one hour to the next. Because his had been a rough, unloving childhood that handicapped him emotionally, he didn't know how to love, or even how to be kind. If he wasn't blaming Mom and me for his woes, he was blaming his father.

With my first dog, Lady - 1951

2

Abuse

About the time I was six years old I began to notice that my stepfather was becoming more verbally abusive toward my mother and occasionally towards me. He was a big guy; six-foot-three and about 235 pounds, and I was very afraid of him. His drunken anger was a normal part of our lives.

Because I was not his real son, he didn't like having me around, and so I became his "whipping boy." The older I got, the more verbally abusive he became toward me. He daily called me names: "bastard," "worthless" or "no better than a piece of dung." Nothing I did ever met his standards. He was extremely critical of my friends, girlfriends, or just the way I mowed the grass. Whenever I messed up, he attacked me personally instead of talking about the offense. I was a "stupid S.O.B.," a "fat ass," or I was "never going to make it in life."

He particularly liked to confront me when other people were around. Word by word, he was destroying what self-esteem I had. It seemed that he wanted me to fail in life, thus proving to the rest of the world that his estimation of me was correct. He seldom offered advice to me because he wasn't really concerned about my future. The pathetic advice he did offer ran along the lines of "get all you can, any way you can."

By the time I was ten years old he was drinking heavily and was physically violent, beating both of us regularly. Mom tried to intervene when he was abusive to me, but her efforts only brought her more beatings. He used everything from a razor strap, belt, coat hanger, and extension cord to beat me with, and once whipped me so hard with a switch that I had cuts all over my legs, and was out of school for a week.

I hated being fearful. When I heard his footsteps coming toward my room I hid under the covers and broke out in a cold sweat. Sometimes he would beat me, sometimes not, but I hated being afraid. The fear caused me to hide in my room when the doorbell rang or when we had company, because I knew he would humiliate my Mom or me. I became introverted and retreated to my room after school to avoid being around him. I was embarrassed to be related to him.

I despised knowing that Mom was being hurt and that I was unable to do anything about it. She'd plead with him, "No, please, don't," over and over, while he kicked and hit her, and I'd be in the next room hearing the entire dialogue. I dreamed of coming to my mom's defense with a gun or a baseball bat. It was truly a miracle that my family survived.

In those days abuse wasn't reported. Years later my mother told me she'd had no idea he was that kind of person before she married him, but once she was in the marriage, she saw no escape. She was already embarrassed because she had been divorced once, which was frowned upon back in the fifties. She did the best she could with what she had, which wasn't very much. We were a very poor family; not that we couldn't have had more. Though my stepfather made decent money as a GM supervisor, he spent most of his earnings on alcohol.

School was a struggle for me from the beginning. Much of my problem was low self-esteem, which stemmed from my shoddy appearance. I was overweight, which naturally brought about teasing from others. We seldom had money for new clothes, so I wore the same shirts and jeans repeatedly. They were constantly being patched and repaired, but my mother always made sure they were clean. My shoes were often so worn out that my toes poked through. Kids made fun of me, and taunted me about why my mother didn't buy better clothes. I didn't really care what they liked or disliked, but I became angry when they talked about my mom, and often got into fights, resulting in my being suspended for a day.

Besides the self-esteem issues, learning was also a challenge for me. I had great difficulty learning to read, because of a lack of training in phonics. I was terrified of being called upon and not knowing the answer. My mother worked in the evenings so I had no one to help me with my homework. Earnest didn't think much of education and took no interest whatsoever in mine. He didn't even think I was smart enough to finish school, often saying, "you'll be nothing but a piece of shit when you grow up. You're too stupid to be anything else."

He wanted me to learn a trade, and suggested that I should become a mechanic. There was nothing wrong with that, as I loved to work on my 1957 Chevy and other old cars. And that's what he did for the most part at GM as a supervisor. But it just wasn't a lot to aspire to.

Between having no emotional family support, and dealing with daily stress, my schoolwork suffered and I was a poor student. As the stress wore on I came to believe that school was no longer important: it was just a place to get away from my stepdad for a few hours a day.

Although Mom had many disappointments in life, she was a consistently loving mother. She tried to make up for the verbal abuse by giving me encouragement. She reminded me to always be truthful, to stay out of trouble, and to be kind. And she told me that if I worked hard, I could make it in life. She often complimented me for being helpful, since I liked to help her do dishes, mop floors and hang out wash. She had hopes that I would one day become a preacher or a doctor. She thought it was important that I be *somebody*, not just a run-of-the-mill guy. Ironically, she looked up to me and wanted something meaningful to show for her life.

At some point in my childhood, a young relative told me Earnest wasn't my real father. I wasn't really surprised, as I had always instinctively felt that he couldn't be my father and have the low opinion of me that his name-calling indicated. Whenever he talked to my mother about me, he always used the reference "your son." I was 14 when he confirmed it bluntly while we were having dinner one night.

Though the abuse from my stepfather was never-ending, and I lived in constant fear of him, there came a time when I was about 11, when God gave me a certain kind of peace that I was going to be okay through it all somehow. I didn't receive any special revelation or hear voices; I just had peace in my heart that I'd be fine.

3

Stress and Salvation

I was thirteen when Mom and I began attending the Flint Baptist Temple church, and one weekend Mom took me to a camp meeting being held there. A couple thousand people crowded the church to listen to Dr. John Zoller from Moody Bible Institute. That night I accepted Christ.

When the meeting was over I met the actor, Red Harper, who was a good friend of Roy Rogers. I knew who he was, having seen him often on the Roy Rogers TV show, and I respected and trusted him. I knew he was a man of God.

He gave me a small New Testament, and wrote on the flyleaf, Proverbs 3:5-6: "Trust in the Lord with all your heart and do not lean on your own understanding. In all your ways acknowledge Him, and He will make your paths straight."

He told me to remember that passage for the rest of my life. I didn't know what it meant at the time, but I did memorize it, and it came to have great meaning for me.

My stepfather, who had no respect for religion, was very angry that we were going to church, and continually tried to demean us for attending. Mom was afraid of his anger, but she overcame his objections, stood up to him and went anyway, knowing she'd later pay for it through his abuse. Though she felt the need and desire to attend church, she once told me she never felt "good enough" to be in God's house. Her feeling stemmed from the stigma of divorce and the general assumption that the divorced person had sinned, when in fact, that was not the case.

Mom bought me a Scofield Bible, and I'd spend hours in my room every night reading it; not so much because I wanted to become holy, but because the stories intrigued me. And of course, hiding in my room and reading kept me out of my stepdad's line of sight. Even so, in the beginning, he would often come into my room and call me names for reading the Bible. Eventually though, for whatever reason, it seemed that if the Bible was open and I was reading, he began to leave me alone.

Through church, I became involved with a Christian youth group, which was an extremely positive influence on my life. They accepted me, loved me, cared about me, and would often pray with me. It was a fun, active group that offered hayrides, ice skating parties, all-night sings, and other wholesome activities. I began to relax and discover that life could be fun and peaceful.

My self-esteem gradually began to improve. Up until that time, I had felt worthless and fearful, and had no real purpose in life. After becoming a Christian and being around like-minded people, I found meaning in my existence and the strength within to believe in a better future by following Christ.

While my self-esteem was improving, my hate for my stepfather was growing deeper. I was going to church, reading the scriptures, and trying to follow the biblical principles, but sometimes the hate overshadowed—not my faith in God—but my ability to be at home and even look at my stepfather. I despised him with everything that lived inside of me. I thought about ways I could hurt him. Now, of course, I thank God that I didn't.

Around this time he started bringing out the guns he owned and threatening us with those. This was something new, and very frightening.

People at church knew some of what we were going through at home, and someone told me I should call the Michigan State Police (who became my real heroes) when my stepfather became abusive. At first I worried that he'd find out I had called, and he would make things even worse for me. The first few times I called, I begged them not to tell him that I was the one who had reported him, and they honored that request. I called perhaps thirty times during the next two years, especially late at night when he had been drinking heavily and was physically abusive to me or my mother. For whatever reason, Mom would not press charges against him, so there was nothing more they could do at the time. But their visit would end things, at least for that evening. Surprisingly, Earnest was very respectful—or more likely, fearful —of law enforcement. They seemed to be the only people he was afraid of. I believe those phone calls saved my life and my mother's more than once. Only God knows for sure.

Though nothing had changed at home, my life was becoming a bit easier to deal with now that I had found Christ and had friends from church. School was still a struggle for me, and overall my grades were mostly "D"s. However, the one bright spot in my high school years was ninth grade, when my grandmother paid for me to attend a Christian school for a year. The class only had thirteen students, and the teacher was kind and helpful. For the first time, I received "A"s and "B"s on most of all my home work. I wished I could have continued in that environment, and now feel I would have been a better student overall if I had.

After my year in Christian school I attended Kearsley High School. I enjoyed playing football, and had several friends, most of whom were black. I mention this because it was another point of contention for my stepdad, since he was very prejudiced against blacks or anyone else who wasn't white or from the South.

My only white friend was Chuck Mattlee who, along with his parents, became like a second family to me. Chuck's mother, Betty, and stepdad, Byron Warwick, were very kind and provided me a bit of sanctuary on weekends. Mom and Betty would work out ways to get me to the Mattlee house for the weekend to give me a break from my stepdad.

Byron was Chief of Detectives with the Flint Police Department, and didn't usually have much to say. He was a cop from the old days: he wore the hat, smoked a cigar and really walked the straight and narrow. He liked me for some reason, though he rarely spoke to me. He used to tell Chuck and me if we got into trouble he would lock us up himself and throw away the key. We were afraid enough of his threat that we behaved. Whether he would have followed through, I don't know, but we didn't want to test him.

Though I never talked about what went on at home, after a couple years of friendship with Chuck, an event came about that brought it to Byron's attention. I was fifteen and still being beaten. My stepdad had used a razor strap on my legs, and I was limping around at Chuck's house that weekend. Chuck asked what was wrong, and pulled up my pant leg. He asked, "Did that S.O.B. do that to you?"

"Yes," I said, and Chuck went to his father. Byron called me down to their basement and had me take off my shirt. He examined the bruises on my back and legs, and asked if my dad had done that to me. "Stepdad," I corrected, and I admitted he had done it, telling him it had been going on for many years. He said, "Son, I'll take care of you. This is the end." He wanted me to know he was going to confront my stepfather, and said, "If he touches you after that, you call me and I'll arrest him myself."

I was a little afraid of that, frankly, because I feared my stepdad would either hurt or kill me or Mom if he knew I'd been the cause of him being confronted or arrested. But Byron assured me that we would not be hurt.

Shortly afterward, my stepdad stuck a gun in Mom's mouth. I called the troopers and told Byron about it. He had officers come out, though he wasn't able to come himself. However, he did follow through with his promise to confront Earnest.

Byron was part owner of a race car track, and was there most weekends. Our family also went to the races often, and the following Friday night we were there. As we were leaving, Byron, Betty and Chuck walked up to us. My stepdad knew Betty, but had not yet met Byron. He reached out to shake hands, but Byron instead opened his coat, showing his badge and gun. Then, using language that would emphasize his point, he lit into my stepfather.

"I understand you've been abusing your son and your wife and I want you to know, that as far as I'm concerned, you're nothing more than a son-of-a-bitch. If I ever hear of you touching them again, I will use whatever means I need to, to make you feel the pain. I will shoot your ass and I will put you in jail and throw away the key. You're on notice as of this moment that I know who you are, I know where you live, and I know what you've done. If I ever hear of one more incident of any kind of violence, I will come looking for you and it's not going to be pleasant." With that, he turned and walked away.

Earnest didn't say a word. I was afraid he'd let loose once we got home, so I went straight to bed. But he didn't speak to Mom or me then, nor for days afterward. He rarely spoke to me for the next three months, and he didn't bother Mom either, though she was still so fearful of him that she continually walked on eggshells. He'd had the fear of God put into him by an old cop whom I still admire today, though he has been gone for many years.

I will never forget Byron for what he did for us, and for his protection. He epitomized what law enforcement should be, and for the most part, what it is. I developed a great love and respect for police officers and all they do to protect those who can't protect themselves. They put their lives on the line for people like me. Byron planted the seeds for me to someday become a cop myself.

I was so thankful that God had brought Chuck and his parents into my life. Chuck was a good friend and always there when I needed someone to talk to. He died at an early age, and I was sad that he didn't get to see more of life than he did.

I was still doing poorly in school. God had helped me through the self-esteem issues, and he also helped me to maintain composure and a sense of humor. But my grades were still suffering.

At sixteen

By the middle of the tenth grade, the tension at home was just too much to handle. My stepfather didn't want me in the house, which made it hard for me to do my homework. I couldn't focus on school, so I quit and took a job at a lumber yard.

Around this time though, my stepdad would make some drastic changes. A friend of his was a youth pastor at the church Mom and I attended. After Mom told the pastor about the treatment we were receiving at home, he paid us a visit and brought the senior pastor along. Together, they convinced my stepdad to attend church. Evidently he saw the light, accepted Christ, and stopped drinking—at least for a while—then continued to drink off and on. But he began to soften, and his life started to level out.

Ironically, instead of being happy about this change, I resented it, because I didn't want him to escape God's wrath so easily. I wanted him to go to Hell for the hell he had put us through. How could God forgive someone like him, just because he'd asked to be forgiven? It seemed so unfair! So as my stepdad progressed in his new life, I regressed. We still had tension in the home, but now I was the source.

People have asked how I got through those years of constant, violent physical abuse. All I can say is, "It's only by the grace of God that I survived."

My mom felt guilty about how I was being treated, and often asked me to forgive her for what he did to me. But I never had any bad feelings toward her. I understood that she was still broken inside; hurt by the divorce from my real dad. She was embarrassed by the fact that she was divorced from one husband and then married to one who turned out to be a drunk and an abuser. She was humiliated by her family's intense dislike of her second husband. They scorned his verbal abuse, his inability to communicate normal words, and the way he acted and treated people.

As a result, Mom tried to avoid other people as much as possible. I didn't blame her, as I witnessed their cold-shoulder attitude toward her. I felt sorry that Mom had to live with such a mean person, but there was nothing I could do about it. It was a situation only she could change, but she didn't want a second divorce on her record. I have never held that against her. She was a very timid lady, but a woman of God. Her spirit was broken, but her love for Christ was not. She often told me she looked forward to being out of this life and joining the Lord in heaven.

4

In the Army Now

After basic training, with the neighbor and Sergeant-Major who had encouraged me to join.

Finally, at seventeen, I decided my mother needed a break from all the tension and strife—especially since now I seemed to be at the heart of it all. Our next-door neighbor, who was an Army veteran, had been sort of a mentor to me. He knew what I was dealing with at home, and one day said, "Let's get you out of town and into the Army."

I told Mom that if she would sign for me, I would join the Army and leave. I felt it would be best for both of us, and I needed to get away from my stepdad.

My friend and mentor took me to the recruiting office, where I enlisted. I remember them asking if I liked to camp out. I said, "Sure, doesn't everybody?"

The recruiter replied, "Then the Infantry is for you!"

I thought of the John Wayne movies I had watched, in which he had played an Infantry soldier. I loved the thought of the Infantry and felt it would be a real challenge.

On the day I left for basic training, Mom took me to the airport, crying all the way. As I was trying to make my way out onto the tarmac to climb the steps to the plane, she continued crying so much that I almost missed my flight. I know it was hard on her to watch me go, but I hoped it would make things easier for her at home.

After a short flight, I was put on a bus headed for Ft. Leonard Wood, Missouri. I felt as though a huge load had been lifted from my shoulders, now that I was away from home and all the tension I'd been experiencing. I believed that anything I might face in the months to come would be easier than what I had been through.

When we reached the army post, the first lieutenant walked out onto a three-foot-high platform to greet us. I couldn't help but notice the gleam of his spit-shined boots, his pants starched to a point where the crease could cut paper. Even his t-shirt looked starched and pressed. Lt. Edward Peeples would be our "dad" for the next five months. And this powerful black man would become a strong influence on the rest of my life.

He began the speech I'm sure he'd given to many other new recruits. "I'm here to teach you how to stay alive, and I promise I'll do the best I can to make sure you know everything I know. Your drill sergeants are older guys who have served in Korea. We'll take care of you and teach you the right way to do things. It'll be hard and some of you might want to go home. If you do what we tell you to, and don't give up, you'll find you can do more with your body and mind than you realize. My door is always open. If you need to talk to me, let the first sergeant know. My policy is, if you want to speak to me, you can speak to me."

We later learned that in most units, recruits had to talk initially to the first sergeant, who would then decide whether or not to allow them to talk to the lieutenant. But Lieutenant Peeple's philosophy was very personal. He truly cared about his soldiers, and was very compassionate.

As he wound up his talk, he said, "I am a soldier just like you. Whatever I ask you to do, I will also do. When you graduate, I'll be there to shake your hand, and you'll be a soldier just like me."

In the entire 5 ½ months of basic training, he never missed a day. Often, while inspecting the ranks, he would stop and talk to individual soldiers personally. He'd ask how we were doing, or if we were writing home regularly. Though he was kind and compassionate, he was also tough. He didn't bend or compromise if someone thought the training was too hard. He pushed them to do more than they believed they could. Still, there were those who didn't make the effort, and were booted out.

It surprised me, and others, I'm sure, that the lieutenant rarely used any profanity. Coming from the background I'd had, of abuse, shouting, filthy mouth, and instability, I found in him the complete opposite of everything I'd known. He quickly became a hero in my eyes, and the epitome of ethics and honor. He once told us, "You need to be the kind of men who will do the right thing even when no one is looking."

I'd remember those words for years to come. Not only did I try to live by that creed, but I used him as an example much later in life when I taught ethics classes to police departments.

True to his word, when we graduated from boot camp, Lt. Peeples attended and shook hands with each one of us. None of us wanted to leave this man. We would have followed him into any war.

Lt. Peeples

Years later I tried to find him, but couldn't. However, I have a picture of him which I keep on my desk. Whenever I look at it today, I still hear his words and feel his influence.

I loved being in the Army, and felt that I'd finally found a purpose in life, by serving God and Country. The men I served with were like family to me. Yes, the training was hard and long, but after I fell into bed each night, at least I felt like I had accomplished something that could be used to help others. I learned more from the drill sergeants than I'll ever realize. They were hard on us and yelled at us to get our attention, but we needed that kind of discipline. Their intent was to train us to listen. If they told us to fall to the ground, we'd better do it; for in combat, if we stopped to ask questions, we'd be dead.

The army—especially the infantry—isn't about us, it's about the team and fighting together as a unit.

After basic training and advanced schoolings, I was shipped out and assigned with the Third Armored Division in Germany. Two years later I was transferred to the Third Infantry Division, also in Germany. My best buddy while in Germany was a guy whose last name was West. But everyone called us salt and pepper because he was black and I was white and we were always together. His color never made a difference to me. My mother always taught me, "God made man in His image, not color." How I wished the world could see that.

Though the military was tough, it was, in my mind, easier than what I had been through at home. I felt free. And what did I do with my new freedom? I began smoking and drinking heavily, though I was aware I was displeasing the Lord. Ironically, I was becoming some of the things I disliked about my stepfather. I still struggled daily with the memories of my early life with him, and with what my mother might still be going through. The turmoil within my soul kept festering. The old fears and nightmares of what he had done and could still be doing to my mother ate at me 24/7. I began to feel that life would never really change in the future. And I was looking for a change.

The Vietnam war was hot in 1966 and most of our platoon volunteered to go. I figured I might as well give my life for a good cause. Not because I thought I was a hero, believe me, but because I felt my life wasn't worth much at that point. So I, too, requested a transfer from Germany to Vietnam. Our sergeant major had other ideas however, and tore up our requests. He was looking out for us, and told us we were stupid to want to go to war, where— being Infantry—we'd surely be on the battlefield.

We were not to be deterred, though, and several of us wrote to Defense Secretary McNamara saying we wanted to go. He wrote back, saying, "I'll send you." McNamara sent notification to the unit that we would be leaving for Vietnam. The sergeant major was angry, but had us do PT for the next six weeks so we'd be in shape. He knew what we were getting ourselves into. Within six weeks I received my orders to the 1st Infantry Division—the Big Red One.

We arrived in 'Nam in 1966. As we disembarked from our plane, we watched body bags being loaded onto the one next to us. Suddenly the gravity of where we were and what we were in for struck us. My friend West was sent to a different squad, and headed off in another direction. I climbed into the back of a truck headed up Highway 13 to Lai Khe. Along the way we could see smoke from air strikes in the distance.

Shortly after arrival in Lai Khe, I met and became friends with PFC Duane Eddy, a strong, outspoken Christian who had been a student at Bob Jones University and wanted to become a pastor when he returned home. He had seen over eight months of constant combat, but was steadfast in his walk with the Lord. He became a mentor, showing me that in the midst of trials, our God can deliver us. He wasn't fearful of combat or death. And it did seem that God was looking over us. During a nighttime patrol with several other soldiers, it was so dark we were holding onto each other's web belts in order to stay together. Some of the soldiers had a bad habit of hooking the pins of their grenades through the front of their uniform. It was convenient, but dangerous. One particular night, one of the guys said, "I think I just pulled my grenade out." We all tensed, waiting for the detonation we knew was coming. But it didn't. When we returned to camp, the pin was still attached, and the grenade was nowhere to be found. We could only thank God for keeping us safe.

On August 25th, 1966, a LRRP (Long Range Reconnaissance Patrol) team, consisting of 15 special recon soldiers, found itself in a Viet Cong base camp. A "May Day" was radioed to the company, requesting help and informing the captain that there could be as many as 900 VC in the camp. The captain sent two platoons—about 120 men—into the enemy camp in seven APCs

(Armored Personnel Carriers) and two M-48 tanks to rescue the team. However, he neglected to inform us of the number of enemy we could be encountering.

The APCs that got us through firefights

When we were within about 25 yards of the road near the camp, we were ambushed. Shock, fear and adrenaline all kicked in, and we began shooting. Two of our APCs were hit with mortar rounds and everyone was screaming for the crew to get out in case it exploded. The VC were shooting from both sides, not caring whether they hit their own men in the crossfire. We lost about 15 men in the first hour.

Eddy and I were in the dirt, and yelled at the sergeant to get the case of 50-caliber rounds off the track, since we'd have to set it on the ground to use it. As the sergeant was pushing the box off with his foot, he saw my helmet under him and yelled to let me know it was coming. By the time I saw it, it was too late. I tried to catch it, but it weighed over 100 pounds. When it hit me in the stomach I felt a ripping sensation in my right side. But I had no choice but to carry on.

One kid had enough sense to call for an air strike, and yelled that we needed it now. Coordinates were set at 20 yards away from each side of the track, and napalm bombs were dropped on top of the VC. The intense heat and the concussion from the hits were terrifying, but we knew it was better than being pinned down and killed one-by-one by the VC.

After the air strikes, we pushed the damaged vehicle to one side and into a clearing where we could turn it around. We then realized we'd played right into the hands of the VC, and now they could surround us. Mortars began hitting around us, so we got into the track and closed the hatch. One young soldier was shot through the chest, but high and to the right. He remained conscious and I started bandaging him. The inside of the track was covered in blood.

In the heat of battle

Packed inside the APC, we were overwhelmed by the smell of blood, the intense 115-degree heat, and the gun powder smoke. We were nauseous and feeling like we would pass out any minute.

Our track commander, having the same issues, opened the hatch to get air. He was immediately hit by a mortar round and fell back down into the track. Blood was flying everywhere. Those of us inside the track could see that only the lower part of his body was left. Someone inside yelled that we should get out, in case the track exploded. Another of the soldiers and I climbed out and were running to find a cover position. We continued firing at the enemy as we ran. Wounded and dead bodies were lying everywhere, along with their M-16s and ammo. We started gathering the clips of ammo, since ours were nearly gone.

Our sergeant major, his left arm nearly blown off, continued firing his .45-caliber pistol. I thought, *what a leader!* He was mad, as I would be. He would eventually be carried out on a medevac dust-off. Months later we heard that he was at Walter Reed Hospital and his arm had been saved. What an inspiration he was and always will be in the hearts and minds of those who knew him.

Someone called for more dust-off choppers, as we had so many wounded, but the helicopters couldn't come in close enough. An Air Force chopper with spring-loaded landing gear was nearby, and was willing to try it. Our Hueys could hold six men, but theirs could only hold two. A full-bird colonel heard our call for help and came in. We saw his chopper get hit and fall straight down from about 25 feet. It bounced and settled, and the colonel got out and started walking toward us. We had to yell at him to get down, as he seemed oblivious to what had been going on in the area. Then he looked around and saw the bodies.

After a ten-hour firefight, our unit was relieved by another division so that we could recover our dead and wounded, set up a perimeter, and dig in for the night. Some of us kept watch while others would try to grab a few winks, though it was difficult to sleep. Eighty percent of our men were dead or wounded, and only eight or nine of us were still able to shoot. We spent the night smoking, hiding the cigarettes under our ponchos so they wouldn't be seen. We shook from the chills, which were caused more from the shock of what we'd been through than from the cold. And for a couple of us, it wasn't over yet.

The next morning, when we were sure the perimeter was safe, we were preparing to leave the area. Several of us began carrying the bodies of our brothers to the track. As we gently loaded them up, a lieutenant colonel strode over and barked, "This is no time for niceties, just throw them up there."

Eddy yelled back, "We're not going to do that; these were our friends and we're going to show them respect."

He could have been charged with insubordination, but the lieutenant colonel wisely walked away.

We had brought all our personal belongings with us from Lai Kai, and I went looking for my things, since my shirt was soaked with blood and I wanted to change into a clean one. Everything was gone. I never knew what happened to it, but it was a bitter loss after what we'd already been through. I'd had a letter from Sandra Dee—a sweet, pretty actress I admired because of her wholesomeness— along with a new camera, and

Taking a much-needed break

several other personal items. There was no sign of any of it. I'd already taken off my bloody shirt, so I grabbed one that was lying on the ground, put my arm in the sleeve and immediately took it back off. It, too, was soaked in blood, even worse than mine had been. I put my own shirt back on.

Eddy and I were walking away from the APC toward a major who would tell us how to get back to base, when I heard small-arms fire. As I turned and looked over Eddy's right shoulder, I saw a flash and smoke, and felt myself being knocked into the air. I landed on my back and knew I had been shot. The bullet entered my upper left arm and exited the back center of my left shoulder. I landed on my arm, and since my shoulder appeared to be a bloody stump, I thought my arm had been blown off.

I called for a medic. I had been right next to Eddy, but now I couldn't see him. A black medic, a sergeant, came over to assist me. Because of all the injuries sustained in the long firefight of the previous day, he had few supplies left. He used cotton balls to pack my shoulder, and saw that the exit wound was wide open, exposing other tissue. Later a doctor told me it was open almost down to my lung.

The medic was able to wrap the shoulder enough to slow the bleeding, and he gave me some morphine for the pain, which was like being on fire. The medic kept insisting, "Look at me," to keep me conscious and focused.

This medic saved my life, and when I finally returned home, I told my stepfather, "Don't ever say anything negative about blacks again, because it was a black medic who saved my life."

When a dust-off helicopter came in, I was loaded on the left side, and then saw Eddy for the first time, being loaded on the opposite side. He had been shot by the same round that got me, and I kept telling him that we were going to make it, to hang on. I realized then how badly I wanted to live. We arrived at the aid station north of Lai Khe, and as we were being unloaded, I glanced over at Eddy. When they lifted him off the gurney, I could see daylight through him. There was a huge open gap where his heart had been. I didn't need anyone to tell me he was dead.

A doctor started an IV and packed the seven-inch exit hole in my shoulder to slow the bleeding. He told me I had a severe wound and could consider myself fortunate to be alive. I was immediately transferred to Ben Hoa 7th Field Hospital near Saigon, where I was examined and advised that I would be transferred to surgery within a matter of minutes. By then I'd had enough morphine that I was wavering and the pain was decreasing.

Through the blur of drugs, I could still hear two doctors discussing the need to amputate my arm. Only then did I realize it was still attached. Since first being loaded into the helicopter, I had been lying on my torn limb to pressurize the injury. I had assumed the arm was already gone. Now I was so glad to realize it was still a part of me, that I refused to lose it. I began to loudly protest amputation, and, afraid I would be tricked into consenting, I became wary of signing any forms. The doctors agreed to do the best they could to save my arm.

On a humorous note, the surgical nurse was talking to me and kept saying, "Look at me and don't go to sleep," which was hard to do, since I was extremely drowsy. Then I heard her say, "Boy, you stink," and that ticked me off. I said, "Well, if you had been in the same clothes for as many days as we have, you would stink too."

She laughed and said, "Good, you're awake!"

During surgery they stopped the bleeding, repaired the muscle and tissue damage, and attempted to wire the exit wound closed. I spent two weeks in the ice box (ICU) to prevent the likelihood of infection. The room was extremely cold, but I was wrapped very tightly in blankets and felt secure. I was heavily sedated with morphine several times a day, so I was not in any pain.

I spent four more weeks on the ward after leaving ICU. The wound was tearing and the wire they used to close the exit wound was doing more damage than good. They removed the wire and changed the treatment to daily packings, peroxide swabs and penicillin. I gradually received less morphine for pain and more antibiotics. A 250-pound nurse from Texas would hold me down by sitting on my buttocks while she swabbed out the wound with bottles of peroxide. It was so painful that if I'd had the strength, I would have bounced her off me.

All this time God was working on me and helping me realize that life is a precious gift. I thanked God for that special time He gave me to stop and reflect on life itself. My awareness of what was going on around me—the cries of pain, the nightmares, soldiers dying on the ward—made me appreciate being alive. I just hoped I'd make it home someday. The uncertainty was an eye-opener to say the least.

One night I could not sleep, so I began to put my thoughts into a poem about the Vietnam war, the war buddies I knew and those I didn't know who wore the uniform; for the many who died and for those who made it home. I completed the first eight verses while in the hospital. Thirty years later, in 1996, I added the last two verses.

Viet Nam 66-67

Today I leave for a foreign land,
Where there is no love for any man.
Where the blood of every man,
woman and child runs deep and cold
And where people die, both young and old.

In this war full of suffering and pain
On whom can we actually place the blame?
But I know what we're fighting for
On that lonely distant shore.
A land full of tears instead of song;
A place where they say we don't belong.

But how do they know?
For they haven't seen
A place that was once so green
Now tainted by the blood of human beings.

We are willing to die here because we think
It's right to walk this land both day and night
To try and help these people to see
That there is a better way through democracy.

These men and women gave of their lives
Because they shared and cared a type of love that's real,
That only comes by having to spill
Some precious blood on a faraway hill.

To demonstrate something that can't be bought
With words, programs, false ideas, or even money,
To some that might sound even funny.

But let me say a thing or two.
I might not believe in the way it was fought
And I cry about the lives that were lost.
But I still wish we had more of them
Who believed that right was better than wrong.

Call it whatever you want,
But real freedom cannot be bought,
And if you're not willing to pay the price
You don't have the right to criticize
Those who gave the ultimate sacrifice.

I thank God to have known
Those men and women who gave of their own
To serve their fellow man far away from home.
God, may we never forget those
who have not returned; MIA's, POW's
The term that we use to try and describe
Those that are missing with tears in our eyes...
But, God, may we stand with them everyday
At our workplace, and especially when we pray.
And, God, thanks for America—a land that is still free.
Free because of men and women You created—like these.

Our prayers are for those who wait—
Their loved ones from that faraway place.

Oh, God, give them strength from your amazing grace,
Strength to know that You're in control
Through the peace that You can give within their souls.
God, may they see Your presence so real
Awaiting their loved ones' return from the field.

I wrote a letter to Dr Billy Graham, asking him to pray for me and that God might use me someday in ministry. He wrote back more than once and gave me a list of Bible verses to read and remember. I still have his letters, 48 years later.

After a month on the ward in Saigon, I was transferred to the 249th General Hospital in Osaka, Japan for skin grafts. I'd spend the next three-and-a-half months there. The wound was healing slowly and the doctors felt that the extensive damage warranted a medical discharge. I didn't want to get out of the service that way because I knew it would hinder my future career choices. After therapy, my only options were to take a medical discharge or finish my tour of duty in Vietnam.

I went back to Vietnam in January 1967 with a totally new perspective. Everyone on the plane was going back for the second time, and this time there was total silence during the entire trip. No jokes or frivolity; now we knew what we were going back to.

Second trip to Vietnam, faking a smile

During the next seven-and-a-half months I was involved in numerous firefights, though nothing as dramatic as the one in which I had been wounded. I was troubled about the possibility of being shot again and was much more cautious. My faith became deeper as I realized that death might be my military legacy.

As a soldier, you try to accept this, even though you're only a young man in your early twenties. This acceptance made you either stronger or bitter. Survival was accomplished hour by hour. When you were walking "point" it was minute by minute (I believe any soldier or Marine who walked the point in combat will agree, it's a very humbling and scary experience.) Every soldier has to take his or her turn while on a combat operation. The mission is to walk about 25 yards ahead of the main body of soldiers, looking for trip wires and listening for movement or strange noises, in order to warn the men who follow. The point man is to try and make contact, to spot the enemy, and communicate their location to the unit, so they don't get caught in an ambush. It is really good for your prayer life, as the old saying goes, "There are no atheists in the fox hole."

I would take it one step further and add that while "walking the point," I read the Bible daily and became more verbal about the Lord and His security. I was not preaching to anyone except myself, while examining my own many shortcomings and faults. I continually thanked God for His forgiveness and security, and that He would not leave me even when people do. That was and is real comfort and hope to go on.

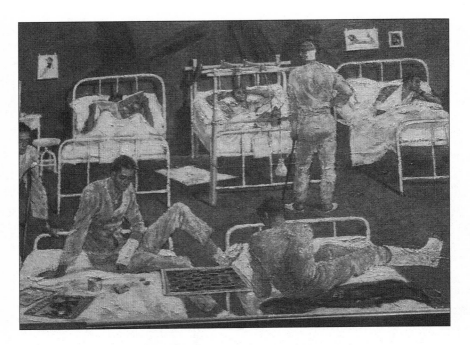

Painting of hospital ward in Vietnam

5

Back in the U.S.A.

I left Vietnam in July, 1967. By this time my stepdad had retired, and my mom had been transferred to Reno, Nevada as a manager for K-Mart. I headed for Reno and moved in with them for a month. I was having restless, sleepless nights, due in part to my experience in Vietnam. Once a person has been shot, that sense of danger, surprise and shock never quite goes away. Family members soon learn to wake someone gently, preferably from a distance. If Mom were to come in and touch me, I'd likely jump out of bed immediately, scaring both of us. Mom understood that I was still having nightmares, and she was gentle and patient.

My relationship with my stepdad was gradually improving. When I was a child, he had never paid me a compliment. The first I ever received from him came about when I was visiting home after my first tour of duty in Vietnam. He seemed to admire me for doing what I felt was right about my military obligation. He bragged to friends that his son wasn't a long-haired draft dodger. Suddenly, I was now his "son." After my discharge he told me he was proud of me and he became protective about my rights.

I was trying to forgive him, but I still couldn't like him. I had often fantasized about my real father and his reasons for leaving. I had one photograph of him and saw that he looked remarkably like me. Now that I had reached adulthood, I began to realize how easy it would have been for my real dad to contact me. The fact that he never did caused me to see that it wasn't in God's plan. So instead of wishing for something I'd probably never have, I tried to think of my stepdad as a father. I prayed for God to change both of us and to begin the healing process. This mindset helped me to accept what I had, rather than try to create something I'd never have. Still, I continued to think of my stepdad as simply a parent, not as a "father."

Mom encouraged me to do something constructive with my time, so I applied for a job with the Reno Police Department. I'd always thought about becoming a cop, and the PDs were hiring a lot of vets, so it was a good fit. I started work on September 1st, barely a month after arriving back home. I know now I should have given myself more time off before jumping right back into another high-stress situation, but at the time I wanted to get out of the house. Though my stepdad and I were getting along somewhat better, I just didn't enjoy being around him. Once I began earning a paycheck, I was eager to get out on my own, so another police cadet and I shared an apartment.

The PTSD hit me one day in an unexpected—and embarrassing—way. I was walking down Main Street in Reno, which was crowded with people everywhere. I thought I heard a gunshot and—thinking I was the target—I hit the ground, looking for cover. People on the sidewalk were looking at me strangely, wondering what had happened. I soon recognized that the noise had only been a truck backfiring. When I realized what I'd done, I quickly got up and made a joke about tripping on a crack. I was thoroughly embarrassed by my action, and I slipped into an alley and tried to recover. I was cold and had the shakes, and I didn't know why. At that time I didn't know what PTSD was all about, and wouldn't completely understand it for several more years.

I was assigned to work in the crime lab, taking and classifying fingerprints, photographing crime scenes, developing prints, etc. Since many of the cops were vets, we shared a common bond. They understood what I was going through, and we became like a tightly-knit family. I was surprised at the reaction of many of our friends and neighbors who wanted nothing to do with me because I had been—in their minds—a "baby killer." The term was ironic, in that I once helped our medic deliver a baby in a village deep in the jungle. The birth took place on a sofa so dirty and stained it would be a miracle if both mother and baby didn't die from an infection. The mom was very grateful and thanked us.

During my second month on the job, I was asked if I'd consider becoming a reserve officer, because of my military training. I was a workaholic, due to my need to keep occupied, and they'd let me work as many hours as I wanted, so I agreed. On my days off from the crime lab, I worked the street during daytime and the paddy wagon at night.

The following May, ten months after returning from Vietnam, I met Jolene, who would soon become my wife. At last—I had a home, a job, someone I loved and who loved me, and goals in life. In 1969, fourteen months after we married, our son was born. Life seemed perfect.

6

Law Enforcement

Around 1970, we moved to Redding, California, so that I could continue my education. After completing my high school requirements, I attended Shasta Junior College and began working toward an associate of arts degree in police science. I loved classes pertaining to law enforcement and was getting good grades.

While still going to school, I worked part time for the Red Bluff PD and full time at the local airport, working security and taking care of the flight school. Whenever I had a free day, I drove the hour-and-a-half to Nevada City to interview with the Sheriff's department for a position there.

During that time, many significant things were revealed as to how God would use me. First, and most importantly, in 1973 I met the man who would become a life-long friend and mentor. Bob Blecksmith and his wife, Sheila, were and are amazing people. When he began to mentor me, I'm sure he didn't realize we'd become friends for life.

In August, 1974, I was hired as a Nevada County deputy sheriff, and our family moved to Nevada City. Now that Bob and I were working together, we became closer friends. We saw each other nearly every weekend, and our families also became close. Bob's three kids were a little older than mine, and befriended them. Bob and Sheila invited us to Calvary Bible Church, which became our home church and would

With friend and mentor, Bob Blecksmith

play a big part in my life during one of our toughest times.

Bob and I were friends on the job as well, and he saved my life more than once on calls where I didn't have enough back-up. One example involved a robbery at a drugstore. The guy had a rifle and was going to shoot me when I came around the corner, but I was down low enough that I could see him. Bob yelled for him to drop the rifle and he did. The guy may or may not have hit me, and may or may not have killed me, but having Bob there was certainly a deterrent.

Bob has the highest ethics of anyone I've ever met, in law enforcement or in the ministry for that matter. He had an amazing influence on so many cops throughout his career, and he was always fair, to good guys and bad guys alike. He was a role model for officers, providing a real-life demonstration of how a police officer—and a man—should act. It's a tribute to him that most of the cops wanted to be more like Bob, and many came to know Christ because of him. He won numerous awards throughout his career, for his work ethics, and for making the most drunk-driving arrests in California.

Bob walked the talk of Christianity. He would pray before a shift, asking God to help us find the bad guys and get them off the street. He held a Bible study group once a week at 6:00 a.m., and encouraged me to become a part of it. I did, even though I often would rather just go to bed after an all-night shift.

While Bob was a mentor to many officers, I saw him as much more than that. He had so many qualities I admired, and was like a father-figure to me, though he's only 10 or so years older than I. The way he treated his wife and kids helped Jolene and I look at our style of parenting and how we treated each other, and we wanted to emulate him. He took the time to teach me how to talk to and treat my son, who was growing up fast.

Bob had an even keel spiritually, and wanted to raise his kids in the community where they had a good church and a good foundation. I know he was passed over for promotion at least once because he didn't want to move his family away from the community he felt was best for them. His family was his priority.

In those first years after we met, Bob was a good friend and mentor. Later I would discover just how great a friend he really was, and the impact a dedicated mentor can have on a person.

I was excited to finally become a street cop, and I was determined to be the best one the department had ever seen. I completed my BA in Criminal Justice at Sacramento State University, attended FBI schools, and completed my basic, intermediate, and advanced P.O.S.T. Certificates (Police Officer Standards and Training.)

In my spare time I taught multi-media first aid and CPR for the county, volunteered for search and rescue, trained a police dog and went to every available seminar and school.

While I was working on my BA degree, the sheriff's office was looking for officers who would attend the deputy coroner school. Of course I jumped at the chance. The instructors were coroners, and we were taught what to look for at a crime scene. It was better instruction than my police officer training had been. As deputy coroners, we would be first on the scene for all death calls.

Nevada County Sheriff's Deputy

After completing the school, I spent the next five years being the night-shift on-call coroner, and handled at least one body a week. Part of the job was to determine whether a supposed suicide was really that or whether it was actually a homicide. Many homicides are staged to look like a suicide, and unfortunately, the murderer often gets away with it.

While my combined duties were often stressful, and I was working long hours, I loved my work and was still looking for new challenges.